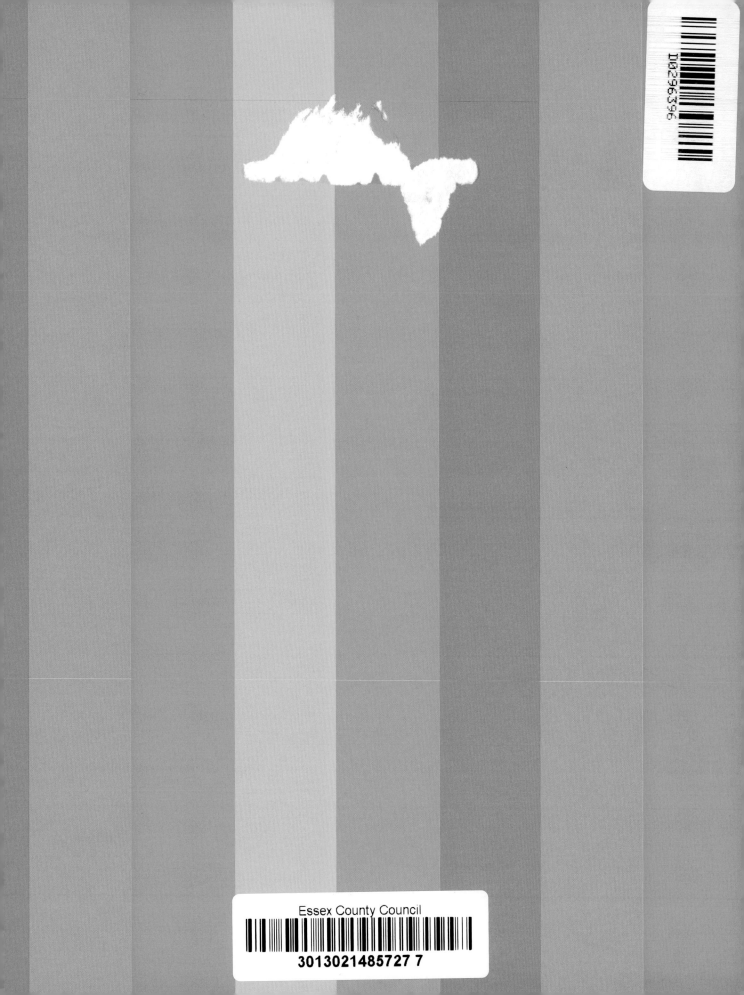

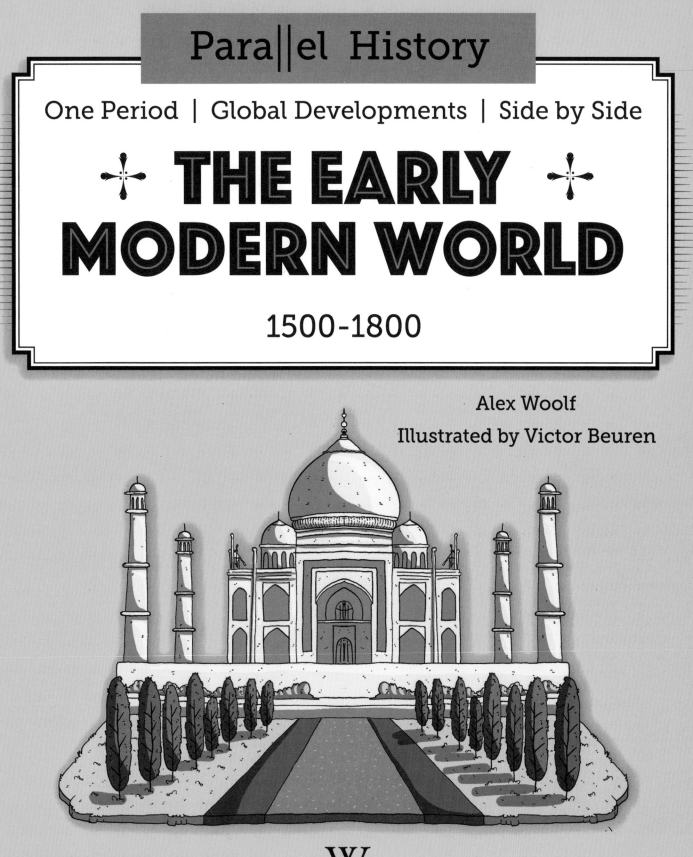

Para||el History

One Period | Global Developments | Side by Side

✣ THE EARLY MODERN WORLD

1500-1800

Alex Woolf

Illustrated by Victor Beuren

W

FRANKLIN WATTS

LONDON • SYDNEY

Franklin Watts
First published in Great Britain in 2017
by The Watts Publishing Group

Credits
Artwork by Victor Beuren
Design: Collaborate Agency
Editor: Nicola Edwards

ISBN 978 1 4451 5740 5

Printed in China

Franklin Watts
An imprint of
Hachette Children's Group
Part of The Watts Publishing Group
Carmelite House
50 Victoria Embankment
London EC4Y 0DZ

An Hachette UK Company
www.hachette.co.uk

www.franklinwatts.co.uk

FSC
www.fsc.org

MIX
Paper from
responsible sources
FSC® C104740

✛ CONTENTS ✛

INTRODUCTION

The early modern era runs from the end of the Middle Ages to the end of the eighteenth century. During this 300-year period, different parts of the world became a lot more interconnected. Largely because of European exploration and colonisation, permanent contact was established between previously isolated parts of the globe. Goods and ideas were exchanged between the 'Old' and 'New World'. This process enriched the European powers, but could be devastating for the indigenous people in the countries they colonised.

Colour Key

- Africa
- Americas
- Asia
- Europe
- Australia and Oceania

British Empire
French Empire
Dutch Empire
Spanish Empire
Portugese Empire

This map shows the areas of the world that had been colonised by different European countries by the start of the eighteenth century.

Europe

The early modern period witnessed enormous economic, cultural, scientific and technological advances in Europe. It encompassed the Renaissance, a revival of art and culture inspired by Classical ideas from ancient Greece and Rome; the Age of Discovery, when European explorers discovered and colonised other parts of the world (see map above); and the Enlightenment, an eighteenth-century intellectual movement based on reason and the scientific method.

Amerigo Vespucci, the Italian explorer who gave his name to the continent of America.

Americas

The colonisation of the Americas, first by Spain and later by Britain and France, was catastrophic for native peoples. It wiped out whole cultures, including the Aztecs and Incas, and killed huge numbers through exposure to European diseases. By the end of the period, European colonies were thriving in North, Central and South America. As their economic power grew, so did their demands for independence.

Suleiman the Magnificent (ruled 1520–1566), longest-reigning sultan of the Ottoman Empire.

Spanish *conquistador* Hernán Cortés meets Aztec emperor Montezuma II at Tenochtitlán, capital of the Aztec empire.

Islamic World

The Ottoman dynasty, founded in Turkey in the 1300s, was an enormous empire by the mid-sixteenth century, but by the end of the eighteenth century it had fallen into decline. In Persia, the Safavid Empire reached its height in the early seventeenth century. India fell under the control of the Muslim Mughal Empire in the seventeenth and early eighteenth centuries.

Africa

In sub-Saharan Africa, European influence grew rapidly, at least among coastal kingdoms, such as Senegal, Gambia and Sierra Leone. The most disastrous aspect of this was the slave trade: vast numbers of Africans were shipped across the Atlantic to toil on plantations in the American colonies. For the many African kingdoms situated further inland, such as Ndongo (in modern Angola) and Monomotapa (in modern Zimbabwe), European influence was minimal and age-old lifestyles continued much as before.

João I of Kongo (ruled 1470–1509) was converted to Christianity by Portuguese missionaries.

GOVERNMENT AND POLITICS

For much of the early modern period, monarchs reigned supreme. Weak or corrupt rulers might be overthrown, but most of the time the authority of European kings, Chinese emperors, African chieftains and Ottoman sultans went unchallenged. In Europe, the period witnessed an increase in royal power, as the strength of the nobility (members of the highest social class) and the Church declined.

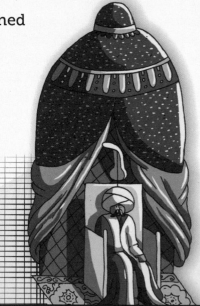

Sultan Selim I being enthroned in 1512. He ruled until 1520.

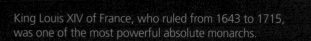

King Louis XIV of France, who ruled from 1643 to 1715, was one of the most powerful absolute monarchs.

Ottoman Empire

The sultan appeared to be all-powerful. Political overlord, military commander, high priest and chief judge, he ruled with God's authority. In reality, however, there were limits on a sultan's power. He could not act without the support of key family members or religious and military leaders. Remarkably, for around 130 years between 1520 and 1651, women of the sultan's harem wielded strong political power, during a period known as the Sultanate of Women.

Europe

This was the age of absolute monarchs. Political power became centralised in the hands of Europe's royalty, as once power-hungry nobles were turned into tame courtiers. The exception was England. In the mid-seventeenth century, Parliament defeated the royalists (those loyal to the king) in a civil war, resulting in a monarchy with greatly reduced powers. By the eighteenth century, Enlightenment ideas of democracy and civil liberties began to put pressure on the absolute monarchs of mainland Europe.

1535 The first Viceroy of New Spain is appointed

c. 1520 'Sultanate of Women' starts to excersise power in Ottoman Empire

King Charles I of England is executed following his defeat in the civil war **1649**

Peasant uprisings weaken Ming rule in China **1627**

China

The Ming dynasty had ruled China since 1368. In the seventeenth century, crop failures and harsh tax rises led to peasant uprisings, and the Ming authority crumbled. By 1659, a new dynasty, the Qing, had risen to power. The Qing created a stronger central government with a Grand Council to advise the emperor on political and military matters.

Americas

Spain's American territories were run by two viceroys representing the Spanish crown. Their authority was limited, however, due to the difficulties of communication over such vast territories, and local governors wielded a lot of power. In North America, Britain's attempts to limit colonial freedom led to revolution — colonists won their war of independence and founded the first modern democracy: the USA.

The Boston Tea Party: in 1773 during the American Revolution, protesting colonists stormed a ship containing a cargo of British tea and tipped it into the harbour.

WAR AND CONFLICT

The early modern period has been called 'the age of gunpowder warfare'. The era saw the widespread use of gunpowder weapons, including cannons, muskets and handguns, both on land and at sea. Soldiers continued to wear metal plate armour until the mid-1600s when it no longer offered protection against more powerful firearms. Gunpowder also reduced the importance of cavalry (mounted soldiers) in battles, though it remained effective in a lesser role until the nineteenth century.

From the seventeenth century, guns and firepower became decisive on the battlefield.

At the Battle of Bushy Run, 1763, colonists fought Native Americans. The colonists suffered heavy losses but were victorious.

Europe

Armies grew in size with the introduction of mass conscription. By 1700, the king of France could put up to 500,000 soldiers in the field, compared to 20,000 in 1550. Wars became increasingly deadly, partly due to gunpowder weapons, but also because enormous armies would lay waste to civilian lands for food. Also, warfare lacked rules, and enemy prisoners were often slaughtered.

Americas

From 1689, Britain and France fought a series of wars for control of North America. In the French and Indian War, France lost all of Canada, handing Britain control of the entire continent east of the Mississippi. Native Americans played a part in these wars, with different tribes helping each side. However, the indigenous people ended up the biggest losers as the colonists gradually drove them from their lands.

1543 A shipment of arquebuses accidentally washes up on a Japanese island; the discovery of these weapons forever changes warfare in that country

Battle of Tondibi: a Moroccan army overthrows West Africa's Songhai Empire **1591** **1603-1623** Shah Abbas conquers most of Mesopotamia

Ming armies repel Japanese invasion of Korea **1592** **1618-1648** Thirty Years War in Europe

1500   1550   1600   1625

At the Battle of Nagashino, the impact of firearms was improved by new tactics, with gunners hidden behind spiked barricades taking turns to fire volleys and reload.

Japan

Gunpowder weapons only came to Japan in the mid-1500s, and the effect was dramatic. At the 1575 Battle of Nagashino, thousands of samurai (traditional sword-wielding warriors) were cut down by lines of men firing arquebuses (a type of musket).

Islamic World

In the 1500s, the Ottoman Turks' use of matchlock muskets and cannons on the battlefield helped them defeat the Safavid Persians (see pages 4-5) and the Hungarians. In the 1600s, the Ottomans' heavy cannons proved a disadvantage against more mobile European armies, as did their reliance on cavalry charges against musket-wielding infantry (foot soldiers).

In 1656 a fleet from Venice in Italy defeated the Ottoman navy in the Dardanelles, due to superior Venetian seafaring skills.

1645-1659 Manchu (Qing) armies complete conquest of China

1701-1714 War of the Spanish Succession

1754-1763 French and Indian War

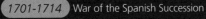

EXPLORATION AND DISCOVERY

The fifteenth and sixteenth centuries were the great age of European exploration. With the Ottomans in control of land routes to the 'East Indies', European powers tried to break into this profitable trade by finding an alternative sea route there. This was made possible by improved map-making, navigation and shipbuilding.

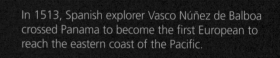

In 1513, Spanish explorer Vasco Núñez de Balboa crossed Panama to become the first European to reach the eastern coast of the Pacific.

In 1488, Bartholomew Dias was the first European to sail round Africa's southern tip and into the Indian Ocean.

Latin America

In 1492 Genoese explorer Christopher Columbus became the first European to make landfall in the Americas since the Vikings. His backers, King Ferdinand and Queen Isabella of Spain, laid claim to this 'New World' and they went on to sponsor missions of exploration and conquest across much of South and Central America – except for Brazil, which was claimed by Portugal.

Africa

During the fifteenth century, the Portuguese launched a series of voyages around the African continent, exploring routes to Asia but also establishing trading bases on the coasts of West and Central Africa. In the sixteenth century, Portugal founded trading bases on the East African coast. During the seventeenth and eighteenth centuries, the Dutch established colonies in southern Africa.

1492 Columbus lands in the Bahamas	*1521* Portuguese expedition establishes first trade contacts with China
1500 Explorers Pinzón and Cabral discover Brazil	*1606* Dutch navigator Willem Janszoon is first European to land on Australia
1513 Juan Ponce de León begins Spanish exploration of Florida	*1606* Russian explorers reach the Pacific coast of Siberia

1500   **1550**   **1600**   **1625**

From 1534 to 1542, French explorer Jacques Cartier was the first to explore Canada's interior.

North America

The Spanish even ventured into North America, as did the English and French, who hoped to discover a North-West Passage to Asia. Italian navigator John Cabot was the first to make landfall, in 1497. The English explored the coasts and inlets of the Canadian Arctic while the French focused on exploring the interior, motivated by the profitable fur trade. The first permanent colonies were established in the seventeenth century.

Russia

During the sixteenth and seventeenth centuries, Russian traders and adventurers began to explore and settle the lands to the east of the Ural mountains. Settlers imposed Russian rule on native populations, enforced by garrisoned *ostrogs* (fortified trading posts defended by soldiers). By 1689, Russia had trebled its territory by expanding across northern Asia.

Yermak Timofeyevich (1542–1584) led Russia's conquest of Siberia.

-1670   French
Lakes re

COLONIALISM

Exploration of the Americas was swiftly followed by colonisation, as the European powers came to appreciate the enormous profits that could be made from mining, farming and trading in the New World. The Europeans also began establishing trading bases and, later, colonies in India and South-East Asia.

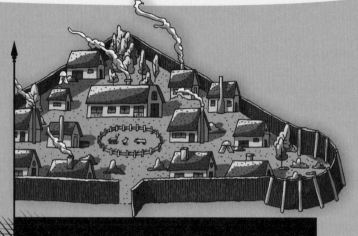

Early American colonists built fortified settlements, like this one at Jamestown, for protection against attacks by Native Americans.

North America

In the late 1500s, England, France, Spain and the Netherlands attempted to establish colonies in eastern North America. By the 1690s, most of the Atlantic seaboard (the region bordering the sea) had been colonised by the French and English. The French had settlements in the north. The English had 12 colonies in what would become the USA. Hostility from Native Americans, as well as the physical barrier of the Appalachian mountain range, deterred expansion to the west.

Spanish America

The Spanish grew sugar and cotton on huge plantations called haciendas. They mined gold and silver. By the 1550s there were some 250 Spanish towns. In the seventeenth century the Spanish came under pressure from rival European powers. The English seized their colonies in Belize and Jamaica. As Spanish power waned, colonists developed a separate identity, creating a new culture that blended native and Spanish traditions.

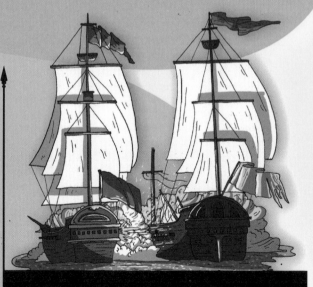

Spanish ships carrying American produce back to Spain were often attacked by privateers – pirates licenced by the English, French and Dutch governments.

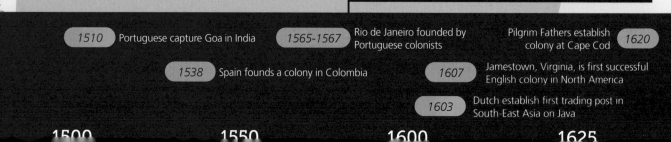

1510	Portuguese capture Goa in India
1565-1567	Rio de Janeiro founded by Portuguese colonists
1620	Pilgrim Fathers establish colony at Cape Cod

1538 Spain founds a colony in Colombia

1607 Jamestown, Virginia, is first successful English colony in North America

1603 Dutch establish first trading post in South-East Asia on Java

1500   1550   1600   1625

South-East Asia

European powers tried to advance their trading interests by influencing the governments of South-East Asian states like Cambodia and Thailand. In the islands, the Europeans tried to break Muslim control of the profitable spice trade. The Portuguese captured the port city of Malacca in 1511. In the seventeenth and eighteenth centuries, the Dutch seized Java, Malacca and the clove-producing Moluccas.

The Dutch city hall in Batavia (modern Jakarta, Indonesia) was a centre of colonial administration, built in 1621.

The British destruction of the French-controlled town of Pondicherry in 1760, shown here, ended French power in India. The stage was set for British rule.

India

European interest in India increased after the discovery by Portuguese explorer Vasco da Gama of a sea route to Asia in 1497. The Portuguese led the way, but they were dislodged by the Dutch, British and, later, French East India Companies. As Mughal authority waned in India, these European companies began to acquire Indian territory, pass laws, administer justice and even wage wars.

SLAVERY

The European colonists who settled in the Americas established plantations growing sugar, coffee, cotton and tobacco. During the 1500s they began forcing people from Africa to work as slaves on the plantations. A 'trade triangle' developed: slaves were sent from Africa to the Americas; the produce of their labour was sent to Europe, and the profits were used to import more slaves from Africa.

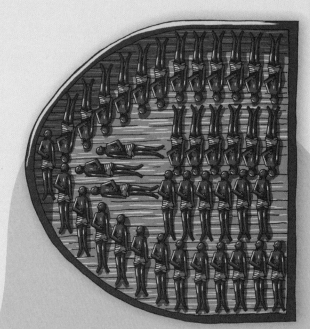

African slave traders with their captives.

Africa

Kingdoms on the West African coast sold slaves to European buyers. The slaves were often from other ethnic groups – prisoners of war or victims of kidnapping raids. Between the mid-sixteenth and mid-nineteenth centuries, Europeans shipped more than 12 million slaves from Africa to the Americas. By the eighteenth century, slaves were Africa's main export.

Atlantic Ocean

Before they arrived in the colonies, slaves had to endure a nightmarish voyage across the Atlantic, known as the Middle Passage. For most of the journey the slaves lay chained in the ship's cramped and filthy hold. Many jumped overboard or tried to starve themselves. Others died from disease.

Over the 300 years of the slave trade, around 2.2 million slaves died during the Middle Passage.

1501   Spain ships first African slaves to its American colony on Hispaniola

1619   First African slaves sold to European buyers arrive in Virginia, North America

Cassava became a valued crop as its roots were a good source of carbohydrate.

Americas

On arrival, slaves were sold to plantation owners at auctions. They were then branded and given a new name. Slaves were forced to work for up to 18 hours a day on the plantations, with no days off. Those who disobeyed their masters were beaten. If they didn't work hard enough, they might be put in neck collars or leg irons. Slaves who resisted or tried to escape were put to death.

Ottoman Empire

Slaves played an important part in Ottoman society. Many were captured in war or enslavement expeditions in Africa and the Caucasus, in South-West Asia, and were then traded at slave markets. Slaves could rise to quite senior ranks in the empire. They could become government officials, harem guards or elite troops. Some went on to become slave owners themselves.

The Ottomans captured European Christian children from rural areas and forced them to become soldier-slaves.

 1655 British Jamaica becomes a major slave market

1660s British colonial assemblies enact slave codes, restricting liberty of slaves and protecting slaveholders' rights

American Declaration of Independence states: 'All men are created equal', but slavery continues **1776**

1787 Society for the Abolition of the Slave Trade founded in London

Northern states of USA, starting with Vermont, ban slavery **1777-1802**

British found Freetown in West Africa, a colony for freed slaves **1792**

FOOD AND FARMING

During the Age of Discovery, explorers brought food crops and livestock from Europe to the New World, and they took New World foods back with them across the Atlantic. This process, known as the Columbian Exchange, has had a worldwide impact on food and farming to this day.

By wearing potato flowers, King Louis XVI and his wife Marie Antoinette helped make potatoes popular in France.

Colonists introduced European farming techniques to the Americas.

Americas

The Europeans brought crops to America that originated in Asia and Africa, such as sugar, bananas, coffee and citrus fruits. These flourished and soon formed the basis of the economies of Latin American colonies. In North America, rice and cotton were grown on slave plantations. Wheat, another European import, became a staple food crop in the Americas. The Spanish also introduced farm animals including horses, donkeys, pigs, cattle, goats, sheep and chickens.

Europe

Many American foods were introduced to Europe in the Columbian Exchange, including potatoes, tomatoes, avocados, chilli peppers, chocolate, maize, manioc, peanuts, pineapples and squashes. Potatoes, in particular, became very important in the European diet. Europeans also benefited from the increased availability of spices from the east, such as cloves, nutmeg, cinnamon, cassia, cardamom, ginger and pepper.

1493-1501 Spanish introduce horses, cattle, sheep, pigs, chickens, sugarcane and wheat to Americas

1520 Tomatoes brought to Spain from Mexico

Portuguese introduce manioc, sweet potatoes, maize and peanuts to West Africa *1629*

c.1525 Portuguese introduce South American chilli peppers to India

1602 Bartholomew Gosnold plants wheat and oats in Massachusetts

Chilli peppers first used in China *c.1550*

1563 John Hawkins brings tobacco and sweet potatoes to England

1500   **1550**   **1600**   **1625**

Tending a cassava crop in Kenya.

Africa

The Portuguese introduced the American crops maize and manioc in Africa in exchange for slaves. These would go on to replace sorghum and millet as the continent's most important food crops. Maize, in particular, thrived in southern Africa. Cassava, a tropical shrub native to Brazil, became another staple crop in sub-Saharan Africa.

Asia

During the 16th century, the Portuguese cultivated crops in India brought over from America, including maize, potatoes, sweet potatoes, chilli, pineapple, papaya and cashew nuts. Sweet potato, introduced to China in the 1560s, helped to feed the nation's growing population, and would become China's third most important crop after rice and wheat.

Portuguese merchants traded animals with the Japanese.

| 1664 | The British East India Company starts importing tea from India to Britain |

| 1631 | Spanish doctor Antonio Colmenero de Ledesma publishes the first recipe for chocolate |

| 1747 | German chemist Andreas Marggraf discovers a method of extracting sugar from beets |

| 1650 | The start of potato cultivation in the Netherlands |

| 1774 | First shops selling ice cream appear in North America |

1675   1700   1750   1800

✛ SCIENCE AND TECHNOLOGY ✛

During the seventeenth and eighteenth centuries, enormous advances were made in science and technology – a period known as the Enlightenment. Europe led the way. China and the Islamic world, which for many centuries had been centres of scientific and technological progress, entered a period of relative decline.

In 1728, Pierre Fauchard (1678-1761) wrote *The Surgeon Dentist*, the first complete scientific description of dentistry.

Britain

Francis Bacon (1561–1626) argued for building scientific knowledge through methodical observation and reasoning, helping to lay the groundwork for the Enlightenment. Isaac Newton (1643–1727) developed the laws of motion and gravity. William Harvey (1578–1657) discovered how blood circulates around the body. Robert Boyle (1627–1691) was a founder of modern chemistry.

Isaac Newton also made key contributions to optics and mathematics.

France

Philosopher and mathematician René Descartes (1596–1650) developed a scientific method based on reason and logic, and made important contributions to geometry, algebra and optics. Blaise Pascal (1623–1662), a mathematician, physicist, philosopher and inventor, built one of the first mechanical calculators. Antoine Lavoisier (1743–1794) discovered the role of oxygen in combustion, and was a founder of modern chemistry.

Netherlands

Gerardus Mercator (1512–1594) was a geographer famous for creating a world map in a style useful for navigators. Spectacle maker Hans Lippershey (1570–1619) was one of the inventors of the telescope. Christiaan Huygens (1629–1695) invented the pendulum clock and made one of the first intensive studies of Saturn's rings.

America

Benjamin Franklin (1706–1790) was, among many other things, a scientist and pioneer in the field of electricity, who invented the lightning rod and bifocal eyeglasses. The physician Benjamin Rush (1745–1813) made contributions to medicine, public health and psychiatry.

✦ ART ✦

This was the age when individual artists became celebrated for their talents. Oil painting was invented by northern European painters, allowing artists to achieve more intricate effects. It was a time of competing artistic movements – the traditional against the new and innovative. In this era of discovery and exploration, different cultures began to influence each other.

An example of Indochristian art. Spanish art instructors taught indigenous artists to paint religious images using Renaissance or Baroque styles.

Paintings like this one in the Mannerist style focused on the emotions, as a reaction to the formal, Classical approach of the Renaissance.

Europe

Artists of the Renaissance, such as Michelangelo, set new standards of excellence. The seventeenth century saw the rise of Baroque, an ornate and elaborate art style employing rich, warm colours. In the eighteenth century, Baroque gave way to the more playful Rococo, known for its pale, creamy tones and graceful curves. The Enlightenment spawned Neoclassicism, a reaction to Rococo, emphasising order and simplicity.

Latin America

In colonial Latin America, artists mixed native art traditions with Christian ideas in a movement known as Indochristian art. Latin American painting was also influenced by the Baroque art of Spain, Portugal, France and the Netherlands.

1430-1600	Renaissance art in Europe
1527-1580	Mannerism in Europe
Early 1500s	Arrival of brass artifacts from Portuguese traders inspire Benin sculptors to create brass plaques with scenes in relief, used to decorate royal palace
1612-1715	Period of the 'Four Wangs', famous orthodox artists in Chinese art: Wang Shimin, Wang Jian, Wang Hui and Wang Yuanqi
1600-1800	Rajput paintings popular in India
1600s	Earliest surviving African wooden sculptures date from this time, created by the Kuba in central Zair

India

The Mughal emperors were great patrons of art, encouraging Persian artists to introduce their styles to India. Persian miniatures, known as Rajput paintings, became popular. They often featured scenes from Indian epic poems such as the Ramayana. Painters collaborated on works until the seventeenth century when artists began to work more individually. Under Shah Jahān (1628–1658), painting became more formal and less personal.

Rajput paintings like this one were popular in the seventeenth and eighteenth centuries.

An example of the art of Dong Qichang, who would deliberately distort reality to create a mood.

China

Dong Qichang (1555–1636) was an influential artist whose work emphasised expression over formal likeness, reflected in his unreal-looking landscapes. During the Qing period, artists were either Orthodox (followers of the ancient masters) or Individualist (followers of Dong Qichang).

1720-1760 Rococo in Europe

1750-1850 Neoclassicism in Europe

1700s The Akan of Ghana start to make small cast copper and bronze weights in form of animals, humans, fruits and abstract geometric shapes

ARCHITECTURE

Traditions of building design changed radically during the early modern period as cultures began to influence each other. The Mughals introduced Islamic, Persian and Turkic styles to India, while European colonists built homes in Spanish, English and Dutch styles in the New World, adapting them for a different climate.

Villa Rotonda in Vicenza, northern Italy, was designed by influencial Renaissance architect Andrea Palladio. It was built between 1567 and 1592.

Europe

Renaissance architecture, with its emphasis on geometric balance and harmony, dominated the sixteenth century. This gave way, in the 1600s, to the ornate and extravagant Baroque, with its curving shapes, twisting columns and dramatic sculptures. In the eighteenth century came the lighter, more graceful Rococo. Another style, Palladian Revival, was inspired by the designs of Venetian architect Andrea Palladio (1508–1580) and featured houses with pillared porticos and domed receptions. The discovery of Roman ruins at Pompeii inspired Neoclassicism, a return to Classical architecture.

Americas

In New England, houses were built mainly from wood in the style found in South-East England. Dutch colonies in what became New York built stone and brick homes in Dutch and Flemish styles. Along the lower Delaware river, Swedish settlers built America's first log cabins. In Latin America, a building style known as Spanish colonial reflected the Renaissance and Baroque designs popular in Spain.

A Spanish colonial house built in 1723 in St Augustine, Florida.

1506 Work starts on St Peter's Basilica in Rome. The biggest building project of the later Renaissance, it wasn't completed until the late 1600s	Taj Mahal built **1630 - 1650**
Palladio begins Villa Rotonda. His work would influence architects for the next 500 years **1567**	Building of the fortress city of Fasil Ghebbi in Ethiopia **1635**
Construction of Selimiye Mosque, Turkey, celebrated for its great central dome and slender minarets **1575**	**Late 1500s** Castles built in Ethiopia during reign of Sarsa Dengel, around Lake Tana region

Japan

Machiya – traditional wooden townhouses – were given new refinements in the early modern period. To protect them from fire, thatched roofs were replaced with tiles, and exposed timbers were plastered over. To cater for a swelling population in the capital Edo (later Tokyo), houses were built with two stories. A popular style for homes was *sukiya*, with its clean, simple design using natural materials.

A *machiya* townhouse.

The Taj Mahal was built as a tomb for Emperor Shah Jahān's beloved wife, Mumtaz Mahal.

India

Mughal buildings featured large, bulbous domes, slender minarets at the corners, vast halls, vaulted gateways and intricate ornamentation. The style reached its peak of splendour during the reign of Shah Jahān. Among the most celebrated buildings are Jama Masjid (one of the largest mosques in India), the Red Fort in Delhi, the Shalamar Gardens in Lahore (in modern-day Pakistan) and the Taj Mahal in Agra.

 c. 1661   Palace of Versailles, the crowning achievement of French Baroque

 1650s   Building of Cape Coast Castle on the Gold Coast (modern Ghana) for holding slaves before they were shipped to the Americas

Work begins on the White House, Washington, D.C., in the Palladian Revival style   1792

1675   St Paul's Cathedral, an example of the more restrained English Baroque

LITERATURE

The invention of movable type printing increased literacy levels and allowed books to be read far more widely than ever before. During this era, the first novels appeared, as did the first operas. Plays were written for entertainment, rather than religious education. However, in some parts of the world, more traditional forms of literature continued to hold sway.

Anne Bradstreet was the first female writer in England's North American colonies to be published. She wrote simple, beautiful poems about home, nature, love and religion.

The famous balcony scene from *Romeo and Juliet* by Shakespeare (c. 1591-5)

Europe

Early modern playwrights including William Shakespeare and Christopher Marlowe (in England), Molière (in France) and Italy's Carlo Goldoni helped reinvent theatre, drawing on traditions of strolling players and *Commedia dell'arte* (Italian travelling theatre troupes) to write realistic human dramas, both comic and tragic. Miguel de Cervantes' *Don Quixote de la Mancha* may have been the first novel. It poked fun at heroic folk legends of the Middle Ages.

North America

Among the first American writers were English adventurers and colonists such as Captain John Smith, John Winthrop and William Bradford, who wrote accounts of their lives to entertain readers back in England. The Virginian planter William Byrd wrote witty, amusing journals. Puritans such as Roger Williams, Thomas Hooker and Cotton Mather wrote stern religious tracts and sermons to instruct and warn their fellow colonists.

1526-1600 Bâkî, one of the most celebrated Divan poets at the court of Suleyman the Magnificent

Ottoman divans were collected in thousands of illustrated, handwritten volumes.

Ottoman Empire

Divan was a style of poetry within the Ottoman Empire. Divan poems explored religious, moral or mystical subjects. Many were allegorical, featuring characters that represented human passions, or they were stories of romantic love that were actually about spiritual awakening. Ottoman prose had to follow strict rules. It was exclusively non-fiction, and it had to rhyme.

Japan

During the seventeenth century, a form of Japanese drama developed called *kabuki*. It was stylised (non-realistic), and performers wore elaborate make-up. Japanese literature was influenced by China and, to a lesser extent, Europe. Ihara Saikaku (1642–1693) wrote funny and cautionary tales that used vernacular (everyday) speech. Also popular were historical romances called *yomihon*.

Izumo no Okuni, who founded *kabuki* in 1603. She began performing this new style of Japanese dance drama in the city of Kyoto.

 1664   *Tartuffe* by Molière

 1719   *Robinson Crusoe* by Daniel Defoe, seen as marking the beginning of realistic fiction

1667   *Paradise Lost*, an epic poem (a long poem about the adventures of heroic or legendary figures) by John Milton

 1759   *Candide*, a highly influential short novel by Voltaire that ridiculed the religion and politics of the time

 1673   Start of *kabuki*, theatre's 'golden age' in Japan

CRIME AND PUNISHMENT

Attitudes to crime gradually changed during the early modern period. Witchcraft, for example, disappeared as a crime during the eighteenth century. Punishments also changed: imprisonment became more common, and mutilation less so. However, for most of the era, punishments remained severe and often brutal, with an emphasis on public shaming, vengeance and deterring others.

Ducking stools were chairs placed on the end of poles and plunged into water. They were used to test if a woman was a witch. If she floated, she was considered guilty; if she sank, she was innocent.

Petty crimes, such as pickpocketing, lying in court or military desertion, were punished with the pillory or stocks.

North America

The Puritans of England's North American colonies imposed a religious law code on their communities. Failure to attend church twice daily was punishable by loss of a day's food, then whipping, and finally six months rowing on the colony's ships. Lying, idleness and bad behaviour were all crimes, punishable by public shaming in the stocks, pillory or ducking stool. Nags and gossips were forced to wear an iron cage on their heads called a brank, or scold's bridle.

England

With a rising population and increasing numbers living in towns, vagrancy (homelessness and begging) became a problem. Highwaymen haunted country roads, and gangs of footpads (robbers) roamed the streets. With high taxes on desirable items such as tea and tobacco, smuggling was big business. Vagrants were whipped and branded on the ear. In England, as in the rest of Europe, those convicted of heresy were hanged. Debtors were thrown in jail .

1547 Boiling alive is abolished as a form of execution in England

The Gunpowder Plot – terrorists plot to kill James I, the king of England, by blowing up Parliament

1605 Jahangir, Mughal emperor of India, establishes his law code, the Twelve Ordinances

1605 The Manchus decree that all Chinese men must shave their foreheads and wear their hair in a long plait **1645**

Plymouth Colony in North America codifies five crimes that carry the death penalty **1636**

India

Under the Mughals, criminals were sometimes executed by elephant. Asian elephants were trained to trample captives underfoot, cut them to pieces with blades attached to their tusks, or torture them over a prolonged period. This punishment was also carried out in other parts of South-East Asia. In Thailand, elephants would be trained to toss victims in the air before crushing them.

Execution by elephant, known in India as *gunga rao*, was banned under British rule.

Ottoman Empire

The Ottoman justice system was based partly on Sharia (Islamic) law and partly on decrees called *kanuns* issued by the sultans. Serious crimes were punished by hanging. These included murder, arson, heresy, apostasy (renouncing Islam), theft of a horse or slave, or disobeying the sultan. Lesser crimes were punished by banishment, amputation of a hand or foot or being forced to serve as a rower in the imperial fleet.

In the Ottoman Empire, people were beaten for being unfaithful to their wives or husbands.

Salem witch trials in colonial Massachusetts lead to the execution of 20 people — **1692-3**

1723 — The 'Bloody Code' starts to be introduced in England, under which many more offences, including hunting deer, killing cattle, setting fire to crops, destroying fishponds or being found in a forest while disguised, carry the death penalty

1683 — The British government grants East India Company the power to establish law courts in India

Taxes on tea and brandy increase smuggling in England — **1700**

The last beheading is carried out in Britain — **1747**

1749 — In Portuguese trading base of Macau, China, Qing authorities forbid any Chinese to convert to Christianity

1675 **1700** **1750** **1800**

✛ RELIGION ✛

The early modern period saw an expansion of Christianity across the globe. Catholic missionaries accompanied colonists and traders to South America, Africa and Asia, while Puritans colonised North America. Jews, ejected from western Europe, established themselves in communities in eastern Europe and North Africa.

The First Great Awakening moved away from ritual and ceremony, making Christianity a deeply personal experience.

In August 1572, a Catholic mob, starting in Paris and spreading throughout France, massacred some 30,000 French Protestants.

North America

The first English settlers in North America were Puritans and Separatists (later known as Baptists) escaping persecution in England. The colonies they established were strongly Protestant. In the 1730s, a religious revival movement called the First Great Awakening began in the English colonies. A minister called Jonathan Edwards preached his brand of Puritanism with great passion, winning thousands of converts.

Europe

The Protestant Reformation was a powerful religious movement that swept through Europe in the sixteenth century. It was driven by a desire to end corruption in the Catholic Church. It led to the splitting of the western Church between Roman Catholics and the new Protestant Churches. Over the following century, bitter wars were fought between Catholics and Protestants in many parts of Europe.

1517	Start of the Protestant Reformation, when German monk Martin Luther begins his protests against Church corruption
First Franciscan missionaries arrive in Mexico — **1522**	**1540** — Start of the Counter-Reformation, the Catholic fightback against the Protestant Reformation
The 'Virgin of Guadalupe' is said to have miraculously appeared, boosting Catholicism among indigenous Mexicans — **1531**	**1561** — A Portuguese Jesuit missionary converts the emperor of Mutapa in Southern Africa to Christianity
King Henry VIII rejects the pope's authority and declares himself head of a new Church of England — **1534**	**1562-1598** French Wars of Religion

Latin America

The Spanish and Portuguese colonists were determined to convert indigenous Americans to Christianity. Jesuit missionaries formed self-governing communities for natives called 'reductions'. The inhabitants had to become Christian, but could maintain their lifestyles. The Jesuits opposed using natives as slaves, incurring the wrath of colonists and leading to the Jesuits' expulsion from the Americas in 1767.

Remains of a Jesuit reduction in Brazil.

India

The Mughals helped establish Islam in India, although the vast majority of the population were Hindu. Most emperors were tolerant of Hinduism, and Hindus achieved high positions in society. But under Emperor Aurangzeb, religious toleration ended. Hindu temples were torn down, their kingdoms invaded and many were enslaved. Aurangzeb also tried to crush a new religion, Sikhism, founded in the late fifteenth century.

Sikh leader Guru Gobind Singh impressed Aurangzeb by writing him a defiant letter in 1705, and the Mughal emperor made peace with him.

GLOSSARY

absolute monarch
A monarch who has supreme authority and is not restricted by written laws, assemblies or customs.

allegorical
Describing a story or poem that contains a hidden meaning.

branded
Marked with a hot iron.

c.
Stands for 'circa' and means approximately or about.

civil liberties
A person's right to be subject only to laws established for the good of the community.

colonisation
The sending of settlers to a place to establish political control over it.

conquistador
A Spanish conqueror of Mexico and Peru in the sixteenth century.

conscription
Compulsory enlistment into the armed forces.

democracy
A system of government in which the people rule through elected representatives.

dynasty
A line of hereditary rulers of a country.

'East Indies'
An old name used by Europeans to describe South-East Asia.

Enlightenment
A European intellectual movement of the late seventeenth and eighteenth centuries, which emphasizes reason and the freedom of the individual rather than tradition.

harem
In former times this was the part of a Muslim household reserved for wives, lovers and female servants.

heresy
A belief or opinion that goes against traditional religious doctrine.

indigenous
Native.

minaret
A slender tower, typically part of a mosque.

missionary
A person sent on a religious mission, especially someone sent to promote Christianity in a foreign country.

mosque
A Muslim place of worship.

movable type printing
A type of printing that uses movable components (e.g. individual letters and punctuation) to reproduce text, usually on paper.

North-West Passage
A sea passage along the northern coast of the American continent connecting the Atlantic to the Pacific, and sought for many years by explorers including Sebastian Cabot, Sir Francis Drake and Martin Frobisher.

optics
The scientific study of sight and the behaviour of light.

orthodox
Following or conforming to the traditional or generally accepted rules or beliefs of a religion, philosophy or practice.

patron
A person who gives financial or other support to a person, organisation or cause.

plantation
An estate or large farm on which crops such as coffee, sugar and tobacco are grown.

portico
A covered walk or porch, typically projecting from the front of the entrance to a building, with a roof that is held up by columns.

prose
Written language in its ordinary (non-poetic) form.

Puritans
A group of English Protestants of the late sixteenth and seventeenth centuries who regarded the Reformation of the Church under Queen Elizabeth I as incomplete and sought to simplify and regulate forms of worship.

Renaissance
The revival of European art, architecture and literature, influenced by the ideas of the Classical World, in the fourteenth to sixteenth centuries.

Safavid Empire
An empire ruled by the Safavid dynasty, rulers of Persia from 1502 to 1736.

staple crop
The main or most important crop in a country or region.

viceroy
A ruler exercising authority in a colony on behalf of a sovereign.

volley
A number of bullets or other projectiles fired at the same time.

FURTHER INFORMATION

Books

Africa and the Slave Trade (Black History)
Dan Lyndon
Franklin Watts, 2013

The British Empire (Great Empires)
Ellis Roxburgh
Wayland, 2017

Ming Dynasty China (That's Me in History)
Bonnie Hinman
Purple Toad Publishing, 2014

The Mughal Empire 1526–1707 (OCR GCSE History SHP)
Michael Riley and Jamie Byrom
Hodder Education, 2017

Taj Mahal (Know About')
Maple Press, 2014

The Ottoman Empire (Life During the Great Civilizations)
Nardo Don
Blackbirch Press, 2004

The Thirteen Colonies (A Look at US History)

Websites

Learn all about the Ottoman Empire:
www.bbc.co.uk/religion/religions/islam/history/ottomanempire_1.shtml

Discover facts about life during China's Qing dynasty:
www.kidspast.com/world-history/0346-life-during-qing-dynasty.php

Find information on the European Renaissance:
www.ducksters.com/history/renaissance.php

Explore the Taj Mahal and learn all about the Mughal Empire of India:
www.pbs.org/treasuresoftheworld/taj_mahal/tlevel_1/t1_mughal.html

This page contains links to some of the most important figures of the Enlightenment:
http://encyclopedia.kids.net.au/page/th/The_Enlightenment

Read all about colonial North America:
www.ducksters.com/history/colonial

INDEX